New SUPER MARIO BROS. WII ™

Simplified Piano Solos

Produced by
Alfred Music Publishing Co., Inc.
P.O. Box 10003
Van Nuys, CA 91410-0003
alfred.com
Printed in USA.

ISBN-10: 0-7390-9115-8
ISBN-13: 978-0-7390-9115-9

TM and © 2009 Nintendo.

Contents

4

NEW SUPER MARIO BROS. Wii

TITLE THEME

Composed by RYO NAGAMATSU

Piano Arrangement by SHINOBU AMAYAKE

Music Supervision by NINTENDO

(Original Key : C)
(Original Tempo : ♩=112)

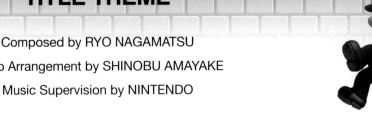

F.O.

NEW SUPER MARIO BROS. Wii
GROUND THEME

Composed by KOJI KONDO and KENTA NAGATA

Piano arrangement by SHINOBU AMAYAKE

Music supervision by NINTENDO

(Original Key : C)
(Original Tempo : ♩=100)

♩≒72

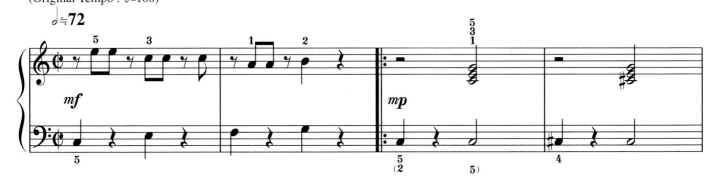

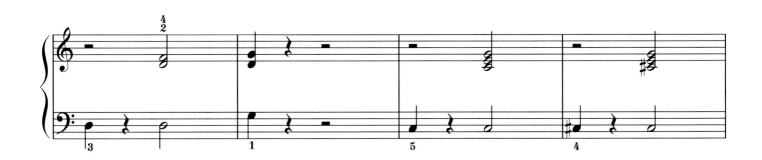

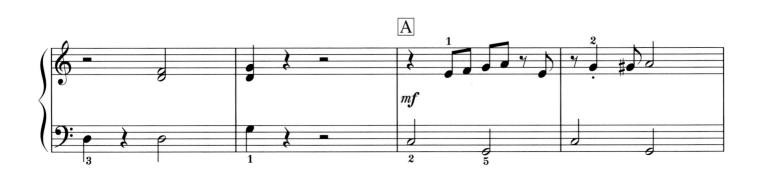

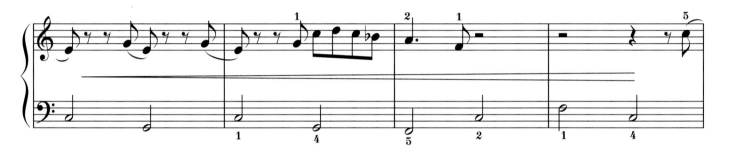

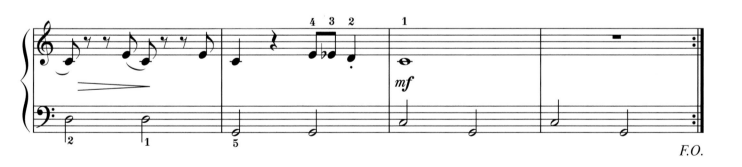

F.O.

NEW SUPER MARIO BROS. Wii

UNDERGROUND THEME

Composed by KOJI KONDO and KENTA NAGATA

Piano arrangement by SHINOBU AMAYAKE

Music supervision by NINTENDO

(Original Key : C)
(Original Tempo : ♩ = 96)

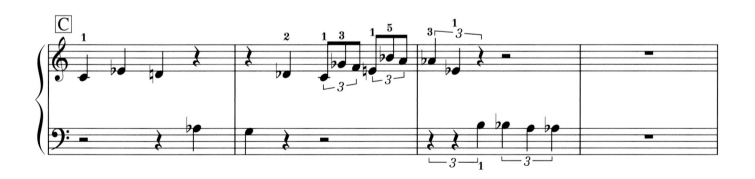

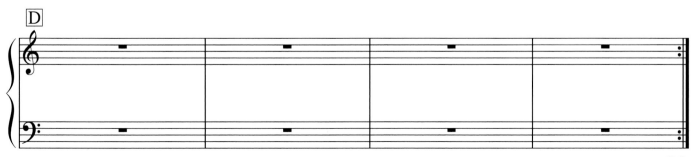

NEW SUPER MARIO BROS. Wii
UNDERWATER THEME

Composed by SHIHO FUJII

Piano arrangement by SHINOBU AMAYAKE

Music supervision by NINTENDO

(Original Key : D)
(Original Tempo : ♩=184)

♩≒132

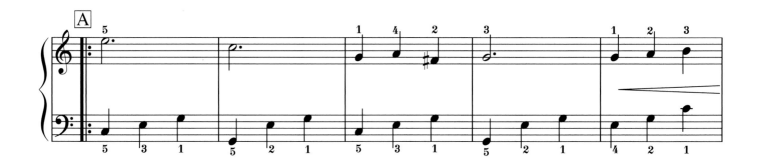

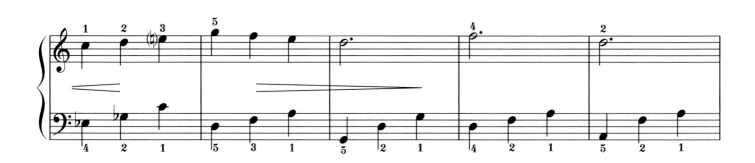

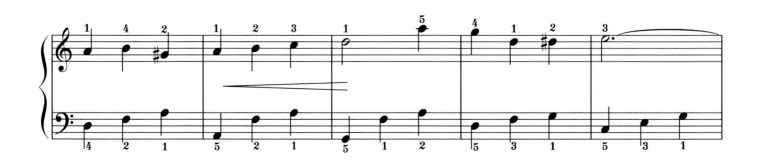

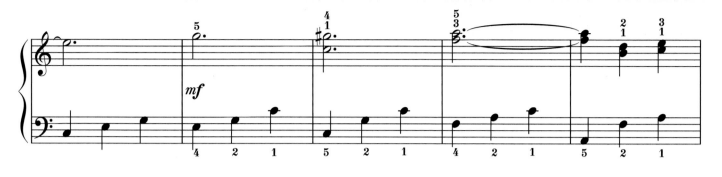

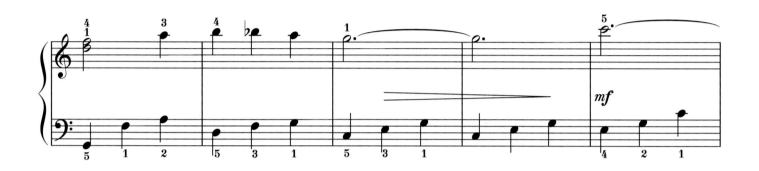

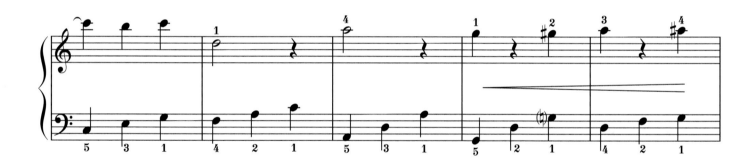

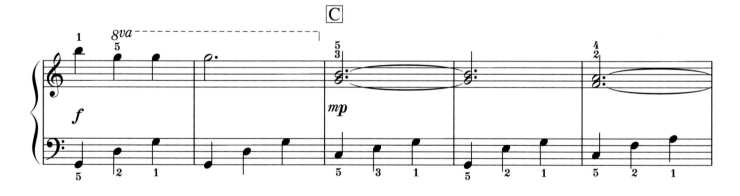

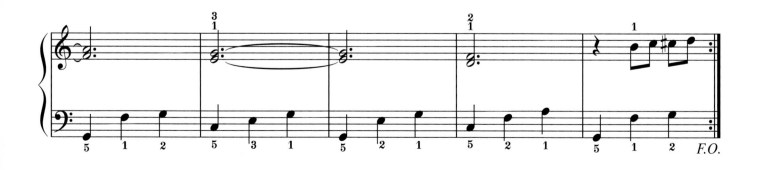

DESERT THEME

Composed by SHIHO FUJII

Piano arrangement by SHINOBU AMAYAKE

Music supervision by NINTENDO

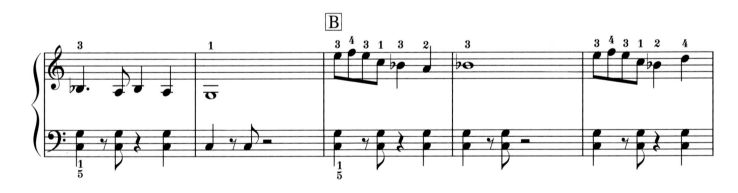

F.O.

NEW SUPER MARIO BROS. Wii

CASTLE THEME

Composed by SHIHO FUJII

Piano arrangement by SHINOBU AMAYAKE

Music supervision by NINTENDO

(Original Key : Gm)
(Original Tempo : ♩=126)

♩≒**108**

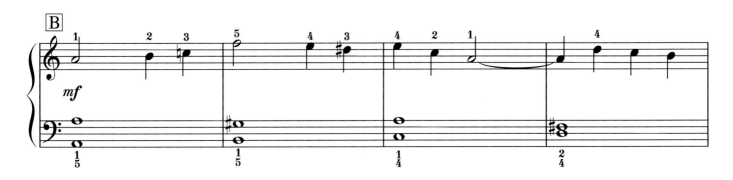

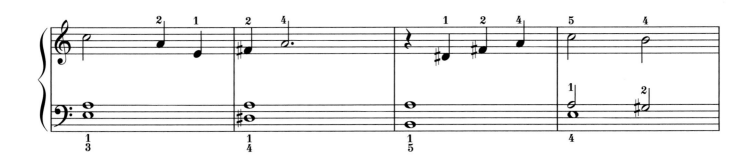

F.O.

NEW SUPER MARIO BROS. Wii

AIRSHIP THEME

Composed by KOJI KONDO and SHIHO FUJII

Piano arrangement by SHINOBU AMAYAKE

Music supervision by NINTENDO

(Original Key : Gm)
(Original Tempo : ♩=114)

♩≒**92**

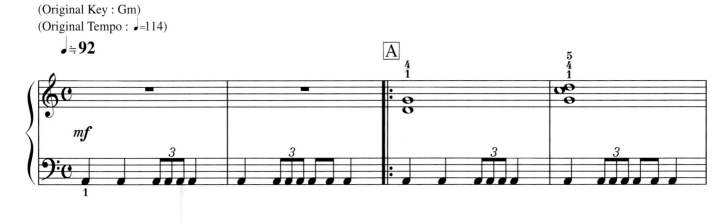

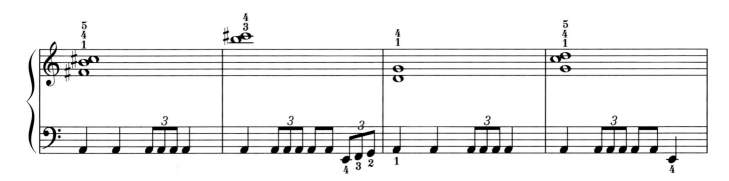

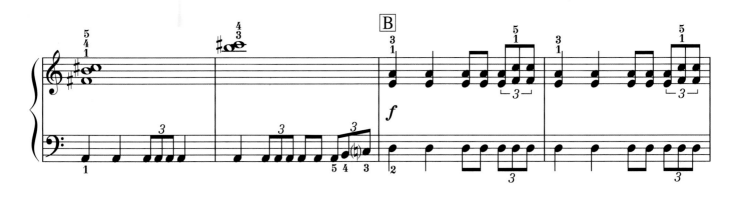

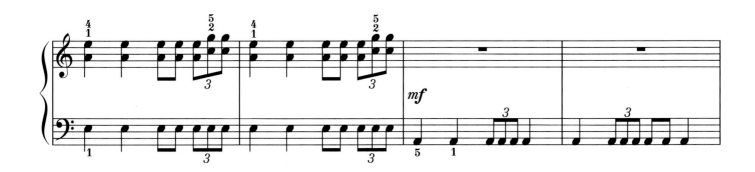

NEW SUPER MARIO BROS. Wii

KOOPA BATTLE 2

Composed by KENTA NAGATA

Piano arrangement by SHINOBU AMAYAKE

Music supervision by NINTENDO

(Original Key : Dm)
(Original Tempo : ♩=162)

♩≒**132**

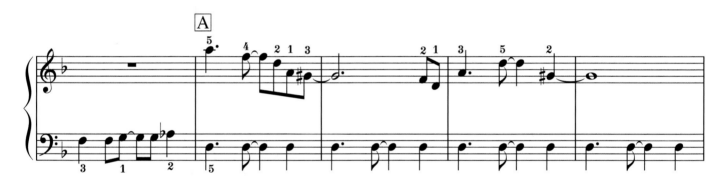

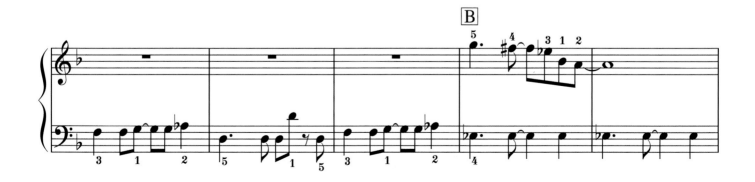

F.O.

NEW SUPER MARIO BROS. Wii
CASTLE BOSS BATTLE

Composed by RYO NAGAMATSU

Piano arrangement by SHINOBU AMAYAKE

Music supervision by NINTENDO

(Original Key : Em)
(Original Tempo : ♩=82)

♩≒72

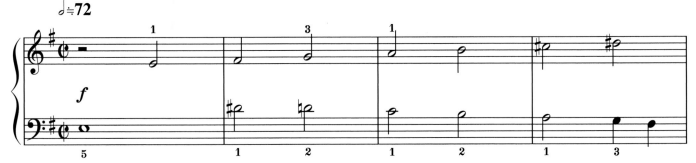

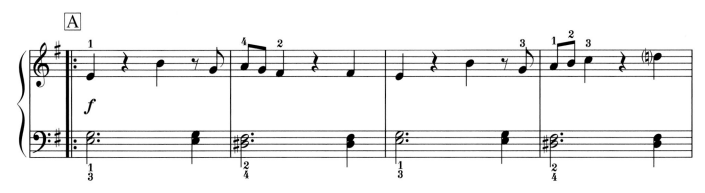

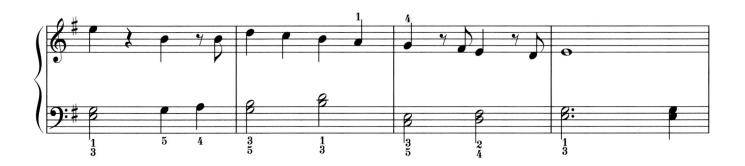

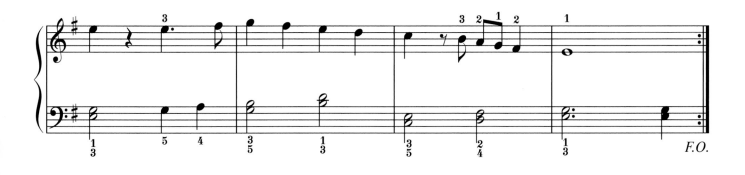

F.O.

NEW SUPER MARIO BROS. Wii
TOAD HOUSE

Composed by KOJI KONDO and SHIHO FUJII

Piano arrangement by SHINOBU AMAYAKE

Music supervision by NINTENDO

(Original Key : F)
(Original Tempo : ♩=118)

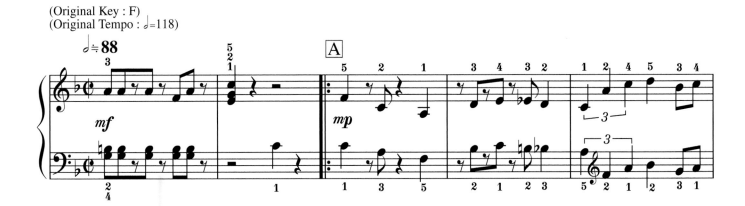

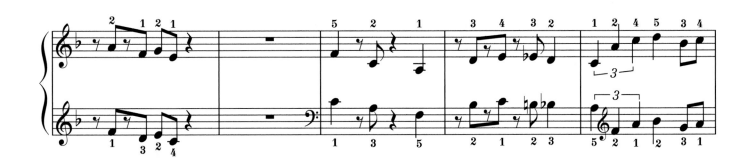

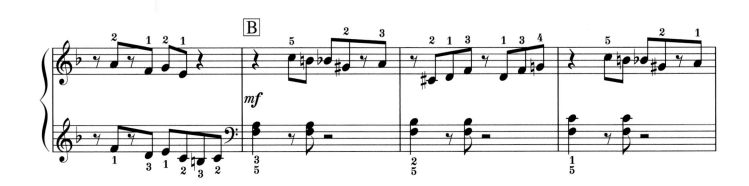

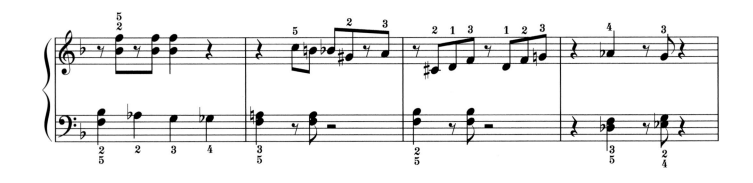

C

D

mp

F.O.

NEW SUPER MARIO BROS. Wii

ENEMY COURSE

Composed by KOJI KONDO and SHIHO FUJII

Piano arrangement by SHINOBU AMAYAKE

Music supervision by NINTENDO

(Original Key : C)
(Original Tempo : ♩=164)

♩≒**112**

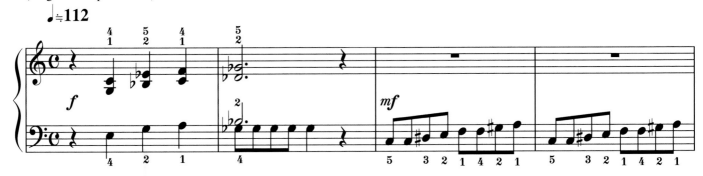

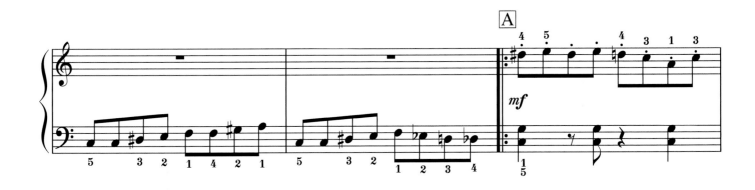

F.O.

NEW SUPER MARIO BROS. Wii

INVINCIBLE THEME

Composed by KOJI KONDO and SHIHO FUJII

Piano arrangement by SHINOBU AMAYAKE

Music supervision by NINTENDO

STAFF CREDIT ROLL

NEW SUPER MARIO BROS. Wii

Composed by RYO NAGAMATSU

Piano arrangement by SHINOBU AMAYAKE

Music supervision by NINTENDO

Coda

NEW SUPER MARIO BROS. Wii
WORLD 1 MAP

Composed by KENTA NAGATA

Piano arrangement by SHINOBU AMAYAKE

Music supervision by NINTENDO

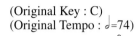

(Original Key : C)
(Original Tempo : ♩=74)

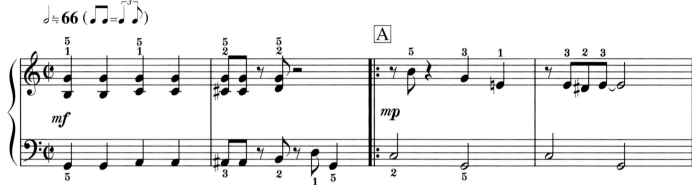

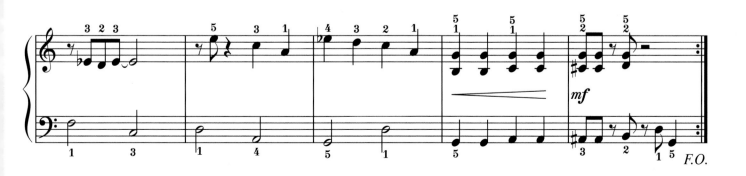

F.O.

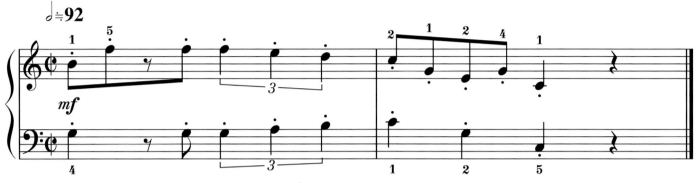

NEW SUPER MARIO BROS. Wii
PLAYER DOWN

Composed by KOJI KONDO

Piano arrangement by SHINOBU AMAYAKE

Music supervision by NINTENDO

(Original Key : C)
(Original Tempo : ♩=108)

NEW SUPER MARIO BROS. Wii
GAME OVER

Composed by KENTA NAGATA

Piano arrangement by SHINOBU AMAYAKE

Music supervision by NINTENDO

(Original Key : C)
(Original Tempo : ♩=106)

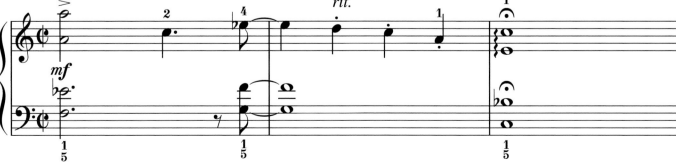

NEW SUPER MARIO BROS. Wii

ENDING DEMO

Composed by RYO NAGAMATSU

Piano arrangement by SHINOBU AMAYAKE

Music supervision by NINTENDO

(Original Key : D → F)
(Original Tempo : ♩=80→88)

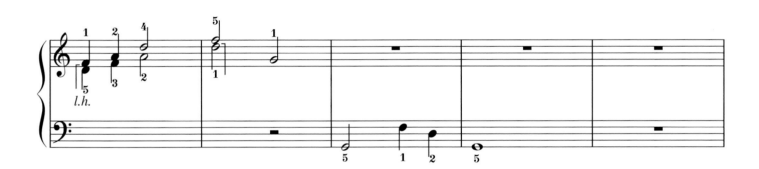

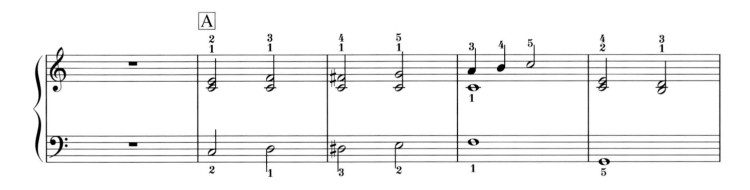

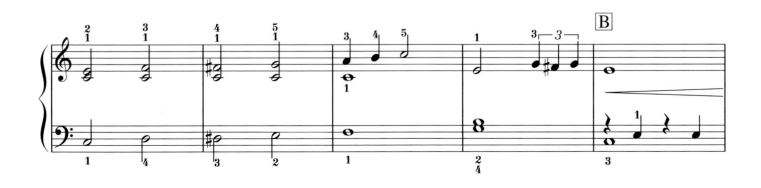